SOAKING 101

Encountering God Series

Book 1

SOAKING 101

FAITH D. BLATCHFORD

ISBN 978-0-615-37544-1

Published by AGE TO COME

www.agetocome.org/www.faithblatchford.com

Printed in the United States of America

Endorsements

If you have ever spent any time around Faith Blatchford, you know she is a walking "God encounter." Her writing style reflects her innocence and intimacy with God. In this book Faith shares her personal journey of learning what it means to "soak" in God's presence. She reveals profound keys in a simple manner that will unlock deeper realms of God in your life. If you are hungering for more of our Father's love and presence, soaking should become an integral part of your life. Whether you are a seasoned "soaker" or interested novice, you will find Soaking 101 to be a stirring and refreshing experience. It left me wanting more of Him.

Joaquin Evans—Director, Healing Rooms
Bethel Church, Redding, California

To those who wonder if it is possible to enter into the presence of Father God, Faith Blatchford has presented encountering God in such a simple way that the reader finishes the book without a doubt that it is easy to achieve entry and as a result reap fantastic returns. Soaking 101 clears away doubts we often have about whether our experience is just our imagination or a real encounter. Faith is a manifestation of time spent soaking in His presence. She oozes the very presence wherever she goes.

Madeleine Tan, Bethel Sozo International
Regional Director, Singapore

Faith has written an encouraging and enlightening book. I recommend it to all Christians who desire a closer relationship with God through spending time soaking in His presence. It comes with practical and creative applications on how to get the most out of your personal time with God. This book will help you learn to experience the fullness of joy in His presence.

Chris Gore – Associate Director
Healing Rooms and Healing Homes
Bethel Church, Redding, California

Faith Blatchford's passion demonstrated in her teaching, preaching and instrumental soaking CDs is to bring people into contact with the power and presence of God. Her new book, Soaking 101, is her latest invitation to encounter God. Whether you are a seasoned soaker or new to the experience, this book will encourage you to "get soaked"!

Dawna De Silva

Founder Sozo Ministry

DEDICATION

This book is dedicated with thankfulness to my Heavenly Father who loved me before I was born, and drew me with His loving kindness until I found my home with Him, in His Presence.

Contents

PREFACE

When I was 8 years old, my dad was diagnosed with cancer. Although my parents were believers, fear brought on by this illness disturbed the peace of our family. The life threatening aspect of the disease brought uncertainty and anxiety.

My life was radically disrupted by this event because we moved to another state for three months during my dad's treatment, and I was placed with my cousins, an hour away from my parents. Although I loved my relatives with whom I was staying, I felt alone and overwhelmed by fear. I knew about God but had no relationship with Him from which I could find comfort.

One day I went with my parents to a healing

service at a church. At the end of the service, the minister invited people to come to the front for prayer. My parents took me with them as they went for prayer. I was unprepared for what I was about to experience.

The minister came to me, looked straight in my eyes and asked me what I wanted. I knew this was serious and had nothing to do with what I wanted for Christmas. After a few seconds of silence, I told him I wanted my dad to be healed. The next thing I knew, he put both his large hands firmly on top of my head. I remember hearing him speak, but have no memory of what he said. I do remember what I felt. Instantly, I was immersed in peace that was tangible. All fear, tension, and worry vaporized in this presence. Although still not a believer, intuitively, I knew I had just encountered God.

That experience set the course of my life. I began a quest to find ways to satisfy the hunger and thirst for God that had been awakened at the healing service. I had become addicted to the presence of God. As I got older, I went to as many conferences, prayer meetings, and church services as I could to be in His presence.

For years I believed the encounters were contingent on being in a certain setting and were determined by God. What a thrill the first time I encountered Him in power, not in a conference or prayer meeting, but in the privacy and quiet of my own room as I invited His presence and allowed myself to be immersed.

In recent years, the word "soaking" has been used to describe an activity that results in the experience I had been having with God. The purpose of this book is to help others who are hungry and thirsty for more of Him, to be filled as they enter the soaking experience. If your heart is beating faster at the thought of an experience that will bring deeper, wider, fuller personal revelation and knowledge of God, I invite you to read on.

FIRST TRY

One of the first times I soaked intentionally was at a conference where a prominent minister was speaking. After the morning session, he invited those in the sanctuary to stay for a time of soaking. I don't think many people in the room knew what he was talking about. I was familiar with the term but had no idea what to expect. At that point I had not connected my private time with God to the term "soaking."

He suggested we find a spot on the floor and lie down, but not too close to anyone else to avoid distraction. I was sitting next to a friend who decided to go to the platform area, thinking she would get more of God closer to the podium and the speaker.

I found a spot on a narrow side aisle wide enough for me and no one else. As I lay down on the floor, it occurred to me I was wearing a dress. The moment I remembered my attire, I noticed someone was lying at my feet. They probably were not focused on me, my dress or what they might see, but their presence was a definite distraction to me. By now everyone had found a place. There was no spot for me to move in order to feel more secure in my dress.

The lights overhead dimmed slightly. This was a welcome change from the blinding glare of the spotlights in the ceiling as I lay on the floor looking up, waiting for further instructions. The minister asked the sound engineer to play some music over the PA system as we "soaked." We had been on the floor long enough to get somewhat settled when peppy praise music blasted through the speakers. All the settled feeling was disrupted as people stuck fingers in their ears to stop the pain. Obviously, the sound man was not familiar with soaking.

After some discussion between the speaker and the engineer, the room was filled with slow, peaceful, music. You could feel everyone's body relax as they recovered from the jarring effect of the previous music.

I got as comfortable as I could on the carpet. Soon I became aware of a musty smell rising from underneath my head. It had been raining and all of our wet shoes had deposited moisture on the carpet. My thoughts jumped from dirty shoes, to germs, cow manure (we were in farm country) and other nasty things that had become attached to the fibers of the carpet on which I was lying. It was too late to spread my raincoat under me as protection.

Not long after the vivid revelation about the carpet, my sinuses started to drain. It had never been my practice to sleep or even lie down without a pillow because invariably my sinuses would open, drain down the back of my throat and trigger a violent and extended sneezing or coughing fit. I knew that neither activity was good in this context. I focused on controlling the tickle in my throat. I hesitated to get a cough drop because of the noise associated with unwrapping it.

At this point, I decided to check my watch. I was sure we had been on the floor at least 45 minutes. Surely this soaking session was about to end. I heard my stomach growl from hunger pains stimulated by the delicious smells coming from the cafeteria. Both from the external aromas and the internal sounds, I knew it was lunch time. Slowly and quietly I lifted my arm and pulled my sleeve back to look at my watch.

Panic gripped me. I felt claustrophobic as I looked at the watch face. It had only been 15 minutes. The speaker hadn't said how long we would be soaking. I was sure he intended to do this for more than 15 minutes. I was trapped. There was no way, in my dress, to climb over people and leave.

As I lay there wondering how much longer we would soak, I realized I should have gone to the bathroom before we started. Once again, I went through mental gymnastics picturing how I could discretely walk over all the people lying in front of me down the aisle, in addition to those in the lobby, and down the long hallway to the bathroom.

In the midst of my panic, I heard stirring and realized the music was fading. I was aware the minister was talking. I don't remember all he said. I did hear him encourage us to try soaking again on our own. He assured us the experience we would have with God through soaking was worth the effort and practice it took to enter in. It occurred to me as I got up that I had not had any awareness of God during that experience. Actually, I had not thought about God at all. Perhaps practice would help me, but I was skeptical. This event had been as far removed from a God encounter as anything I could have possibly imagined.

Because I trusted the speaker and the testimony of his experiences with God, I was willing to try soaking again. My hunger and thirst for more of God's presence motivated me to try something that seemed silly and proved to be unfruitful the first time. My hope was that the next time I tried soaking, I would have the same encounter with God that he had. I was not disappointed!

SO WHAT IS IT?

$\mathcal{D}$efinitions of the word soaking are helpful in order to understand what to expect from the experience. Webster's Dictionary defines the word to soak as:

to lie immersed in liquid (as water); become saturated by immersion; to penetrate or affect the mind or feelings; fill thoroughly.[1]

Soaking can be synonymous with "prolonged immersion" and "complete absorption."[2]

Synonyms of "soaking" include: absorb,

---

1   soak (2010) In *Merriam-Webster Online Dictionary.* Retrieved March 26, 2010, from http://www.merriam-webster.com/dictionary/soak.
2   ibid

assimilate, immerse, marinate, permeate, saturate.

Now that we know what the word soaking means, what does it mean in terms of a believer's life? Very simply, it means to spend time with God, allowing our whole heart, soul, and mind to be immersed, saturated, permeated, penetrated, marinated, filled, and totally absorbed with His presence.

Unfortunately, religion has often put a strait jacket on the believer's heart and soul. A Christian's experience of God has been limited to the mind. Passion in relationship to God has been viewed as almost obscene. Duty has replaced devotion. Living from the mind makes it virtually impossible to obey Jesus' command recounted in three of the four Gospels where He sums up the Christian life by instructing us to love God with all our heart, soul, strength and mind (Matthew 22:37, Mark 12:30, Luke 10:27).

The context for soaking must also be taken out of the religious exercise category. It is not a duty to be performed, nor does it earn favor or points with God. It is a pleasure to be enjoyed. God's intention from the beginning was that we were to live in pleasure. The Garden of Eden means the Garden of Pleasure, of Bliss, of Heaven. Jesus is the door, the way back to Eden.

Soaking is one road back to Eden, where we can be immersed in His presence, experience the fullness of joy, and the pleasure of His company with every cell of our being.

INTIMACY-THE GOAL

A good analogy when thinking about soaking is the experience between a bride and bridegroom. Intimacy between husband and wife is the foundation on which a strong, healthy, fulfilling marriage is built. A marriage relationship that neglects or withholds this type of communion will suffer. Intimacy doesn't just happen even in the best marriage. Both husband and wife may desire intimacy, but it takes effort and determination to protect this area of the relationship from intrusion. It means schedules, offenses, children and even ministry cannot be allowed to rob the couple of the life source of the marriage – intimacy.

Intimacy is, at the same time, both scary and

ely satisfying. Part of the intimidation stems
fear of the rejection that may occur because of
the level of transparency and vulnerability necessary
for this depth of relationship. It is easier and safer to
settle for less in a relationship than to trust oneself
to another so openly—even God—and risk pain.
However, for the courageous, there is strength and
confidence as two become one. I Corinthians 6:17
promises "he who is joined to the Lord is one spirit."
Through the interaction and intermingling of my
spirit with His, I am built up, nourished, cherished,
protected and healed.

A friend of mine became a widow after forty
years of marriage. She and her husband were best
friends before they were lovers. They did everything
together, not because they had to, but because they
wanted to. They lived in a house that had a lovely
garden tucked into a mountainside. A long driveway
traversed the hillside through rhododendrons and
azaleas to the house. Often they would be snowed

in during the winter, unable to drive down the steep road from the house. Their children were no longer living at home, but they never felt alone or isolated, even in the winter, because they had each other.

The day Sam, her husband died, she heard the Lord say, "Live as if Sam was still here, as if you were still married." She got up the next morning, made the coffee, set a place at the table for herself and Sam just as she always had. When she sat down to have her coffee and read her Bible, she looked over at Sam's place. Instead of seeing Sam, she saw the Lord having coffee with her.

From that day, her soaking time was every morning at the breakfast table. She knew how to draw from the Lord the love she needed and to pour out on Him her love, just as she had done for forty years with her husband. Even when the snow in winter kept her shut in on the mountain, she was never alone.

Although we may not have had such an intimate relationship, or even a model of such personal interaction with another human being in terms of communion in mind, emotions, and spirit, we have the opportunity, by soaking in God's presence, to receive what we may not have had in past relationships. The experience of soaking not only expands our knowledge of God, but will enable us to deepen our relationships with others as we experience healing in His presence and the opening of the depths of our being in trust to Him.

God's intent for us in relationships is to start by loving Him in response to His love, then to love ourselves and finally others. (Mark 12: 30 – 31). Experiencing immersion in His love during a soaking session makes loving myself and others much easier and even fun.

DISTRACTIONS

One of life's greatest tests is the ability to overcome distractions. They come in all forms, at all times, and often from the most unlikely person. Sometimes the cause is just random. Other times the impetus is from the enemy.

Jesus had His share of interruptions, roadblocks, and surprises to knock Him off balance. He recognized men and women are sometimes not in tune with Heaven's timing, which can cause disruptions. When Peter tried to dissuade Jesus from His mission, He identified the source and said to him: "Get behind me, Satan!" (Matthew 16:23).

Soaking will not be enjoyed without anticipating the reality of possible distractions. The key to victory is to be proactive. Do not let the distraction take you by surprise. To do this requires taking some time to think through your responsibilities, daily schedule, and environment to assess possible conflicts. An easy action to start with to stop some interruptions is to turn off the phones. Sacrifice may be required such as getting up early before the known daily interruptions begin. Jesus got up early and He didn't even have a wife, children, or phones to deal with.

If you have babies or young children, it is possible to include them in a short soaking time or nap time soaking with you. Older children understand Mommy and Daddy time when they are not to interrupt. They can learn Mommy or Daddy and God time as well. What we place value on our children will place value on as well.

Often the most intrusive distractions come

from within. It is easier to turn off the phone than to turn off the internal voice. Often, as I begin to soak, I find myself thinking about 10 things I need to do later. I always have a pad and pen with me to jot down those random thoughts that come to mind.

Sometimes those thoughts may be a reminder or revelation from the Holy Spirit. Jesus spoke about the role of the Holy Spirit as the one who would bring back to the disciples' minds the things He had said. I believe He not only brings to mind the word of God, but also helps by reminding me of things I need to do. I call this holy distraction.

Other internal and more intense thoughts stem from unresolved issues in my heart such as resentment, anger or hurt. Sometimes guilt, shame, or self-condemnation I feel towards myself may surface. It is good to deal with those issues at the beginning of the soaking time if possible. Left unresolved, these thoughts may tempt me to pull away from God rather than press into Him. The more I know Him through soaking, the easier it is to deal with issues and the less fear I have of coming into His presence "just as I am."

We do not have to be perfect before we can enjoy His presence. We are changed by encountering Him. His light dispels any darkness in us. The point is not to allow any internal issue to distract, or separate us from Him.

Regardless of the source of the interruption, ask Holy Spirit to quiet anything from outside or from inside that would rob you of soaking in His Presence. Let the shalom of God rest like a blanket over any disturbances.

A SOAKING PLACE

When a bride and groom go on their honeymoon, the place is important. It does not need to be a five star hotel, but it needs to have two important components: privacy and comfort. That may be found at the Ritz Carlton Hotel or in a cabin in the mountains with no running water or electricity. Everyone has a different picture of what comfort and privacy should look like.

Jesus had His "place." Although He didn't own a home, He would go into the mountain at night to be with His Father. For the Passover, an intimate time with His disciples, he chose a particular place and had it reserved to ensure privacy and comfort for the last supper (Luke 22:9-12).

Communion with God is possible anytime and in any environment. However, there is benefit in setting aside a specific place. If the spot is familiar and has good memories of past encounters, it will take less time to get settled and focus on God.

The place needs to have privacy unless it is a time of corporate soaking as in a church or prayer house setting. This does not mean a locked door, but simply a place that is separate from the normal flow of traffic in a house or outdoors.

When a bride and groom choose a location for the honeymoon, all the senses are taken into consideration. A cabin next to a garbage dump would not create an atmosphere conducive to romance. The bride in the Song of Solomon describes their bed as being "like a forest glen. We enjoy a canopy of cedars enclosed by cypress, fragrant and green" (Song 1:16-17, The Message Bible).

This description involves sight, smell, and touch. One can even hear the stillness of the forest. God gave us our five senses, as well as our spirit, not just to train them to encounter the things of the world, but more importantly to experience Him.

The sights, smells, and touch that awaken our senses, also prime us to sense Him in every dimension of His being. Our soaking place should not be offensive to any of our senses. Even if all we have is a small room, it is possible to carve out an area that is comfortable and peaceful.

For several years I shared an apartment with friends. I had a small bedroom upstairs. The room was crammed full of stuff including my desk, keyboard, recording equipment, bed, dresser, and comfortable swivel rocking recliner chair. On the wall facing the chair I hung a large picture of a huge beautiful lake with a dock extending into the midst of it. I would sit in the chair and face the picture. Soon I found myself no longer hemmed in by the four walls of my tiny little room but "outside." The picture was an invitation drawing me deep into His presence, as if jumping off the end of the dock into the water.

One evening I decided to soak lying on the floor in my bedroom. There was not a lot of room on the carpet, but enough to stretch out without my feet or head touching the furniture. I got my pillow and lay down. As I was trying to settle on the hard floor, I was aware of the Lord beside me. I heard Him remark to Himself, "This is so uncomfortable. I don't know why people do this." Of course, I laughed out loud and told Him I agreed. I promptly got up and sat in my recliner. I am sure He is happy on the floor with those who like the floor. He just wants to spend time with us.

It is not necessary that your place or position

look like mine. The point is, however we position ourselves in whatever space we have, we are to be comfortable and feel some privacy. Religion would make us think that if we do not set up the soaking place in a certain way, making it almost like a shrine, we will not experience His presence. The truth is, His presence makes any place holy. Even an obscure, dirty stable was sanctified and filled with God the day Jesus was born and lovingly placed in the manger.

SOAKING AND SOUND

*A*ll of life is made up of sounds. Within the womb, as well as from the moment of birth when we let out the first cry, we experience sound. Even alone in a remote area, it is not possible to remove all sound. The sound of our own breathing can be distracting.

It may be that absolute silence only occurs during the half hour referred to in Revelation 8:1 when the writer says "there was silence in heaven". The question is not whether to have sound or not while soaking. It is a question of what kind of sound you choose.

If the sounds around you are distracting, it makes choosing sounds more important. Ear plugs, noise canceling headphones or sound machines are all practical ways to deal with unattractive sounds in your soaking space. Playing music is another way to deal with any disturbing sounds in your environment.

The Bible story about David playing for King Saul testifies to the calming effects of music. David played his harp for Saul, causing the evil spirit to leave and peace to return (I Samuel 16:2-3). Studies from science and medicine have shown the beneficial effect of certain sounds on the human body or mind.

I prefer to listen to music without words when soaking because the words distract me. As a composer, I have created and recorded my own soaking music without words. In addition, music with a slow tempo helps me relax in His presence.

After the first CD was produced, I did some research about music therapy. I learned some music used in therapy has a tempo with less beats per minute than the human heart rate in order to help the body rest and de-stress. Most of the tracks on my first CD were exactly that. The Holy Spirit knows what we need!

Not everyone responds to the same type of music. Some people prefer music with words because the images described help them stay focused. Other people like a faster tempo to keep them awake. Although there are obvious benefits to being awake, sleeping while soaking does not detract from the encounter with God. The Shulamite woman in the Song of Solomon states: "I sleep, but my heart is awake" (Song 5:2). You may not be conscious of what took place while you slept. The outworking of the encounter between your spirit and God may not be evident for weeks, months or even years. However, it is impossible to interact with God and not be changed.

Another form of sound for soaking is water. Ezekiel wrote God's "voice was like the sound of many waters" (Ezekiel 43:2). The sound of water may be a stream, rain, ocean waves, waterfall or a fountain. God built into those sounds a restorative power. We are made up of 50-65 % water. It would be natural to have an affinity for the sound itself since water is so much a part of our makeup. When Jesus described the Holy Spirit within us, He spoke of the Him as a river of living water (John 7:38).

The sounds for soaking may also be your own voice singing to Him, softly praying in tongues or in English. This is not a time for warfare prayer, but for words of love and adoration. In the stillness, it may be the sound of His voice singing to you, praying for you, telling you how much He adores you. According to Hebrews 7:25, Jesus "lives to make intercession" for us. How comforting to hear

Him pray for us as we soak in His presence.

In Psalm 46:10 we read, "Be still, and know that I am God." This verse does not mean close your ears and cease to be conscious. It means, stop talking and fidgeting enough to allow Him to get a word in. The power and sound of His voice, the voice that spoke the world into being, that called Lazarus from the tomb, that spoke forgiveness to the woman caught committing adultery still speaks today. In the quiet place of soaking in His presence, He calls us out of our traumas, sin, and sickness, into our destiny.

Soaking 101

THE FOCUS - GOD

Now that you have designated a soaking place, proactively dealt with anticipated distractions, experimented with sound that is best for you, it's time to refocus on the purpose. All the preparation brings us back to where we started — intimacy. The goal of this time is to enjoy Him and allow Him to enjoy you.

Perhaps that last sentence jarred you. Many of us have had a warped view of God because of our religious background or personal experiences growing up. Even if we know the Bible, we may not be sure of how He feels about us personally. All the goodness, kindness, patience, longsuffering, forgiveness we read about may be for someone else more deserving.

Because of such uncertainty, often we put up defenses when we get near Him, afraid of correction, discipline, judgment, or even rejection. The truth is, He allowed His Son to take our sin and be brutally punished to the point of death for it, so nothing could separate us from His overflowing love for us. We are His delight and joy.

Religion and society are so task-oriented and performance driven that much of our time with God focuses on a "to do" list for God. We are motivated and driven by the subconscious list of requirements needed to be checked off in order to receive from God. We set up our own rules of engagement with God. If I do a certain number of things for Him, I can expect to receive some particular blessing from Him. Even if He is present, we may not experience Him because according to our rules, we don't deserve to.

We are more focused on the list than on Him.

Conversely, we usually have a list for God. We itemize the things we need Him to do for us, our family, friends, nation or the world. This list can be as distracting as the one we have for ourselves. Picture a bride and groom on their honeymoon, enjoying a romantic setting of candlelight, flowers, 1,000-count Egyptian cotton sheets, the sound of the ocean waves crashing outside the balcony. In the midst of this bliss, the bride pulls out a notepad with a list of things she wants her husband to do at the house when they get home. Equally bad timing would be the husband pulling out the checkbook to go over budget cutbacks because of a financial shortfall. The last thing on either of their minds at that moment is the "to do" list or the budget.

It is not necessary to bring the "to do" list or the checkbook to the soaking time. He knows everything on the list as well as how He will handle it. He has counted every penny in the bank and has a plan for paying the bills. It is permissible to relax. The word "be still" in the Hebrew language means "relax." The psalmist wrote that in His presence "is fullness of joy" (Psalm 16:11). Anything that hinders us from fully enjoying His presence should be excluded from the soaking session.

However, soaking is not an emptying of the mind as in the form of meditation practiced by followers of Eastern religion. It is neither mindless nor emotionless. Rather, it is the filling of our mind, body, spirit, and emotion with His presence. It is our time to "lean on His breast" as John did (John 21:20) and for our "heart to burn within us" as did the disciples when they encountered Jesus on the road to Emmaus (Luke 24:32). The result of such communion may result in others commenting that they can tell that we have been with Jesus, just as people remarked about the early disciples (Acts 4:13).

Soaking should be as pleasurable as spending time with your best friend; the person with whom you feel totally at ease, knowing they love you as much as you love them in spite of all your quirkiness and imperfections. When you are together, you aren't watching the clock or waiting for the meeting to be over, but rather ignoring the clock because you are having so much fun talking, laughing, and just being together. You leave feeling encouraged, refreshed, strengthened, loved, and empowered to face your challenges even though you didn't talk about the problems or how to deal with them.

Soaking 101

YOUR TURN

*I*f this is your first try, remember how disappointing my initial experience was. The point is to take the first step. Begin in faith with determination to continue trying until you discover Eden and encounter God on every level and in every aspect of His being and yours.

Having made provision for possible distractions, which includes turning off the phone, adjusting the lights, temperature and sound, select a pad, pen, and Bible, get comfortable in your chosen spot, and begin.

As you start, you may invite the Holy Spirit

to lead you on this adventure. Jesus left Him with us as a source of comfort but also as a guide who would lead us into truth (John 16:13). When we ask for the Holy Spirit's leading we don't need to be afraid or worried about what might take place. He will not take us down the wrong path. As Jesus said, if we ask for the Holy Spirit, we will receive Him, not a scorpion (Luke 11:11-13). So, too, if we ask the Holy Spirit to lead us, He will not take us into darkness, but into light.

You don't need to close your eyes, particularly if you have a view from your soaking spot, or a picture on the wall or a music DVD. If it is distracting to have your eyes open, then close them. This is about what is most comfortable for you. There is no right or wrong way. At this point, you may want to talk to Jesus, consciously turning your heart towards Him, inviting His interaction with you. He is not shy about responding to such a request.

One day in class at a school of ministry I attended, I experienced the power of this act. The teacher was speaking to the class about learning to engage the presence of God. He said that throughout the day he turns the affections of his heart towards the Lord inviting Him to come. As he spoke, I knew he was actually doing what he was saying. As he said "the presence of God comes," I felt God's powerful response to those words. I was sitting on the back row, and was knocked back in my chair by the force of His presence entering the room.

As you invite Him to make Himself known, you may be distracted by thoughts of tasks you forgot to do. Having a pad with you enables you to make a note for later. This is not sacrilegious. The presence of God will not be offended and leave.

You may suddenly feel uncomfortable, guilty, or ashamed. The name or picture of someone who hurt you may come to mind. If so, ask Holy Spirit to show you the issue with the person or anything else you need to deal with. Ask Him to forgive you for any sin He shows you, and as He does, forgive yourself.

You may not be feeling well physically as you begin to soak. It is not necessary to be at your best whether physically, emotionally or spiritually. He is the One who gives us what we need.

One morning I woke up feeling badly both physically and emotionally. I was living alone having recently experienced the loss of my mother who had been my best friend and strongest encourager. It was a struggle to get out of bed. I finally dragged myself to the couch and pulled out my Bible, pad and pen, hoping to receive enough momentum from God to start the day.

I desperately wanted someone to comfort me; to be strength in this painful time. Although I wanted someone with flesh and blood with me, I found myself asking the Lord to pray for me. The next thing I knew, I sensed His presence and felt His hands on my head. I could "hear" Him praying for me, not audibly, but inside. I leaned into Him and felt immersed in peace, comfort, rest, love and hope. That soaking encounter was life-changing and life-giving.

No matter what the issue you need to talk to Him about, do so out loud. Let this encounter be more than merely in your mind, although your mind and imagination will be engaged. If you are in a corporate setting you can speak softly enough not to disturb others, but loud enough to hear yourself.

As peace returns to your mind and heart, re-focus on the Lord. If you are listening to music with words, you may find yourself concentrating on some aspect of the Lord described by the music. If a Scripture comes to mind, ask Holy Spirit to give you deeper revelation; to make it personal and applicable to you. If you receive a Bible verse at this point, it is probably for you, not your wife, husband, child, friend, boss or pastor. Ask the Lord to give you understanding and revelation. Let your heart, emotions, body, all your senses, as well as your mind be open to His words and His presence. The disciples felt burning in their hearts as they encountered Jesus on the road to Emmaus. (Luke 24:32). This was more than a mental revelation.

In 2 Corinthians 2:15, we are spoken of as the fragrance of Christ to God. From that Scripture, it would appear Jesus Christ must have a pleasant smell. As He breathes you in, try breathing in His fragrance. You may be surprised some time by what you smell! He is not limited in the ways He can reveal Himself.

Expect visual impressions or pictures on the canvas of your brain. The Holy Spirit uses your voice, tongue or breath to pray in tongues. He wants to use your mind, the place where you envision things, where you "see dreams" to give you pictures during the soaking time. If you see something that doesn't mean anything to you, ask Holy Spirit what it means. Be like a child; ask a lot of questions. God does not become irritated by our inquiries into His mysteries. He is thrilled we are interested.

The Holy Spirit is resident within us for many reasons. One of His activities is to help us discern spirits. Sometimes we become more adept at discerning evil spirits than we are at discerning the presence of God. The enemy loves to distract us by enticing us to focus on him rather than on God. Psalm 68:2 says the wicked perish at the presence of God. The more time we spend in the glory, the place of the fullness of joy, the less we will be sidetracked by the demonic.

I have purposely not quoted from authors other

than the Bible, or even made a list of suggested books to read. We each need to establish our own personal interaction with God that is not colored by or compared with anyone else. Just as a young couple needs to set up their own home, separate from their parents, we must set up our home in God. How boring if everyone's home looked exactly the same; or if all our experiences in His presence were identical. The God who gave each one of us a unique fingerprint intends to give us a tailor made history with Him. One size does not fit all.

There is no set amount of time for a soaking session. The focus is not on the event but on the presence. Once you are immersed, saturated, marinated, you take Him with you. The fact that the time is up does not mean you leave and He stays. He goes with you, in you and on you. That is why people remarked that they knew the disciples had been with Jesus (Acts 4:13). The experience we have soaking allows others to encounter Him as they interact with us because a part of Him gets on us as we spend time together.

As you soak, may you enjoy His presence as much He enjoys yours. May you be satisfied with the fullness of His joy. May you see Him dancing over you and hear His voice as He sings to you (Zephaniah 3:17). Welcome to Eden!

THINGS TO DO LATER

_____

_____

_____

_____

_____

_____

_____

_____

_____

_____

_____

_____

SCRIPTURE VERSES

_____

_____

_____

_____

_____

_____

_____

_____

_____

_____

_____

_____

_____

_____

_____

JOURNAL

_____

_____

_____

_____

_____

_____

_____

_____

_____

_____

_____

_____

_____

_____

Instrumental Soaking CDs
written/performed and produced by Faith Blatchford

Available at: www.ibethel.org or www.itunes.com

- *AGE TO COME*

- *MYSTERIES*

- *AGE TO COME* – *Vol. 3*

- *BE HEALED!*
  instrumental healing encounter with Scripture

Teaching CDs - available at

www.ibethel.org web store

- *ON THE ROAD TO DESTINY*
  teaching series with Dawna DeSilva

♥♥♥♥♥

Additional copies of

SOAKING 101 can be found at www.ibethel.org

♥♥♥♥♥

Check out www.faithblatchford.com :

Resources For Further Soaking

look for the release of

HEARING 101, Encountering God Series – Book 2